Geography Zone: Landforms™

LAKES

Emma Carlson Berne

PowerKiDS press™

New York

Published in 2008 by The Rosen Publishing Group, Inc.
29 East 21st Street, New York, NY 10010

First Edition

Editor: Joanne Randolph
Book Design: Julio Gil
Photo Researcher: Jessica Gerweck

Photo Credits: Cover © iStockphoto.com/Kasia Biel; p. 5 Shutterstock.com; p. 7 © iStockphoto.com/ Andrew Dierks; p. 9 © iStockphoto.com/gioadventures; p. 11 © iStockphoto.com/Rebecca Dickerson; p. 13 © iStockphoto.com/Liz Leyden; p. 15 © iStockphoto.com/Kyle Maass; p. 17 © iStockphoto.com/Wilfried Martin; p. 19 © iStockphoto.com/pomortzeff; p. 21 © AFP/Getty Images.

Library of Congress Cataloging-in-Publication Data

Berne, Emma Carlson.
    Lakes / Emma Carlson Berne. — 1st ed.
        p. cm. — (Geography zone : Landforms)
    Includes index.
    ISBN 978-1-4042-4208-1 (lib. bdg.)
    1. Lakes—Juvenile literature. I. Title.
    GB1603.8.B47 2008
    551.48'2—dc22

                                        2007038764

Manufactured in the United States of America

Contents

Lakes are basins, or bowl-shaped places, in Earth that are filled with water. Lakes are surrounded by land on all sides.

Lake water is generally fresh, not salty like ocean water. Some lakes in the world are salty, though. They are called salt lakes. Very large lakes are sometimes called seas. Some of the biggest lakes in the world even have waves and tides like the ocean!

The world's biggest lake is called the Caspian Sea. It is in Asia. The Caspian Sea is 149,190 square miles (386,400 square km). That is just a little smaller than the state of Texas.

Lakes, like the Caspian Sea, shown here, are beautiful places. They also give us freshwater and are home to many plants and animals.

Lakes can be formed in many ways. Earth's surface is made up of many large, moving pieces, called **plates**. Sometimes, these giant plates slide up against each other or move away from each other. These movements can make **depressions** that later fill with water.

Glaciers can make lakes, too. As glaciers move, they can cut away giant pieces of rock and dirt. This causes low places to form. These low places become lakes when they fill up with water.

People also make lakes. People use bulldozers and other machines to dig big holes in Earth. Later, the big holes fill up with water.

Lake Michigan is one of North America's Great Lakes. Made by glaciers, it is the United States' largest freshwater lake.

A Pond or a Lake?

Ponds are little lakes. **Scientists** do not agree about how small a lake should be before it is called a pond, though.

Some say that ponds are less than 10 acres (4 ha) across and lakes are more than 10 acres (4 ha). Other people say that ponds are less than 20 feet (6 m) deep.

People in different parts of the world have different ideas about what a lake is and what a pond is. The only thing everyone agrees on is that a pond is smaller than a lake.

This pond has lots of lily pads and other plant life growing in it. These plants help make food and homes for fish and other animals.

Some lakes have salty water instead of freshwater. These are called salt lakes. Usually, salt lakes exist in deserts. The water is sometimes even saltier than water in the ocean.

Salt lakes are created when naturally salty water flows into a lake and cannot flow out another side. Some of the water evaporates, or leaves the lake as a gas, but the salt is trapped in the lake.

Salt lakes sometimes evaporate and disappear. The salt is left behind after the water dries up. This salty land is called a salt flat.

The Great Salt Lake is a well-known lake in Utah. The Great Salt Lake is three to five times saltier than the ocean!

Big, Deep Lakes

Rift-valley lakes are huge, deep lakes. They are formed when two of Earth's plates move away from each other. A depression forms in Earth's surface. This depression is called a rift valley. After a while, the rift valley can fill up with rainwater and water from under Earth's surface.

Africa has many large rift-valley lakes. Lake Nyasa is in the country of Malawi. The lake is an important **resource** for the people who live nearby. Ships carrying cotton, rubber, and rice sail across Lake Nyasa every day. People catch fish on the lake and bathe in its waters.

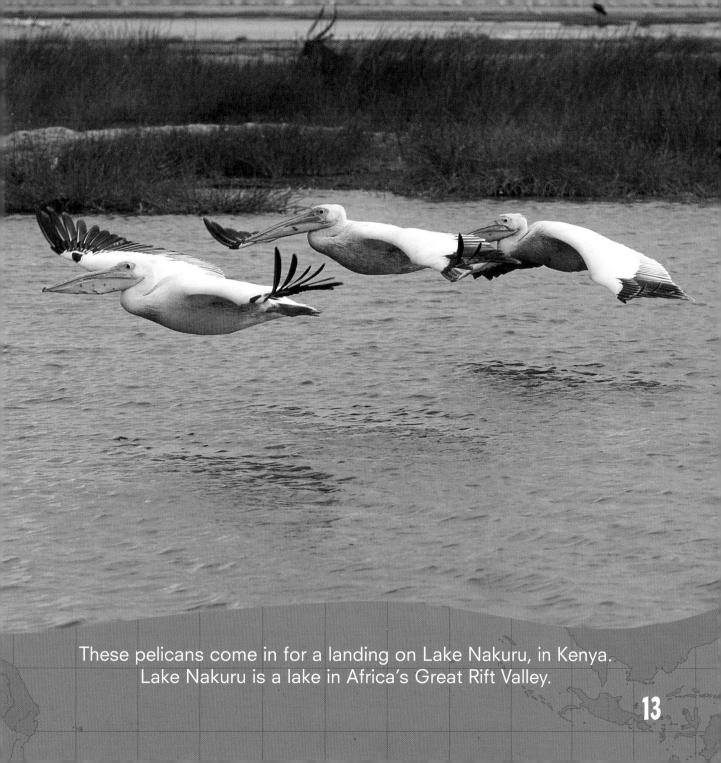

These pelicans come in for a landing on Lake Nakuru, in Kenya. Lake Nakuru is a lake in Africa's Great Rift Valley.

The world has many different kinds of lakes. Some lakes are in **craters**. They are called crater lakes. Under the surface of Earth, there are hollow places filled with a hot bubbling matter called magma. Sometimes, the rock above these places caves in. A deep hole, or crater, forms. Later, the crater fills up with water. Sometimes crater lakes form in the tops of **volcanoes**.

Some lakes exist underneath glaciers. They are called subglacial lakes. The lakes are made of water but they are covered with the glacier's thick ice. The lake does not freeze, or turn to ice, because the ice on top of it keeps it warm.

This crater lake sits on top of Poás Volcano in Costa Rica.
There are two crater lakes on this volcano.

Lakes are very good habitats, or homes, for many living creatures. On the edges of lakes, tall grasses and cattails wave in the wind. Dragonflies fly just above the surface of the water, and bugs called water striders walk on the water's surface. Salamanders and frogs hide in the grasses and under stones at the edges of lakes. Ducks and geese paddle through the water looking for food.

Beavers build their dams in small lakes and ponds. Otters swim and fish. At sunset, many other animals, such as deer, foxes, wolves, coyotes, and raccoons, come to lakes to drink.

Dragonflies, like this one, make their homes near lakes. They fly and dive near the top of the water, eating bugs as they go.

Lake Baikal, in Siberia, Russia, is the deepest lake in the world. It is 5,315 feet (1,620 m) deep.

Lake Baikal is a rift-valley lake. In fact it is one of the deepest rift valleys on Earth. The rift is growing, too. It gets wider by about 1 inch (2 cm) each year. It is also one of the oldest lakes on Earth. It was formed 20 to 25 million years ago. **Hot springs** and mountains surround it. Salmon, whitefish, huge sturgeon, and seals all live in the lake. Many people live near Lake Baikal and use it for business. Because of this, the lake is very polluted, or dirty.

Lake Baikal has one-fifth of all the freshwater on Earth. Here we see Olkhon Island, the largest of the lake's 22 islands.

The Siberian people use Lake Baikal for many activities. Every day, fishermen bring in boatloads of fish to sell. The woods around the lake are used for cutting **timber**. There are also important **mines** along the shores of the lake. Many people have jobs in these mines.

People also come to Lake Baikal to bathe in the hot springs on the shore. People like to sit in the hot water bubbling from Earth and look at the huge, icy lake, the dark pine trees, and the mountains far in the distance.

Here a woman sells fish on the shores of Lake Baikal.
There are 56 kinds of fish living in Lake Baikal.

People all over the world count on lakes for fresh drinking water and for fish to eat. They use the trees around lakes to build homes and other buildings. People can hunt the ducks and geese that live on the lakes.

People also enjoy lakes for pleasure. They have fun swimming and sailing boats on lakes. Many people think that lakes are very beautiful to look at. They like to build houses right on the edges of lakes.

Because people use lakes so much, many are polluted. People must work to keep their lakes clean.

Glossary

craters (KRAY-turz) A large hole on a moon or planet, such as Earth.

depressions (dih-PREH-shunz) Places on Earth's suface that are lower than the land around them.

glaciers (GLAY-shurz) Large masses of ice that move down a mountain or along a valley.

hot springs (HOT SPRINGZ) Places where naturally heated water comes out from the ground.

mines (MYNZ) Pits or underground tunnels from which stones are taken.

plates (PLAYTS) The moving pieces of Earth's crust, the top layer of Earth.

resource (REE-sors) Something that comes from nature and that can be used or sold, such as gold, coal, or wool.

scientists (SY-un-tists) People who study the world.

timber (TIM-bur) Wood that is cut and used for building houses, ships, and other wooden objects.

volcanoes (vol-KAY-nohz) Openings in a planet, such as Earth, that sometimes shoot up hot, melted rock called lava.

Web Sites

Due to the changing nature of Internet links, PowerKids Press has developed an online list of Web sites related to the subject of this book. This site is updated regularly. Please use this link to access the list:
www.powerkidslinks.com/gzone/lake/